Geckos Don't Blink!

Kelly Tills

Copyright © 2021 Kelly Tills
Paperback Edition

ISBN: 978-1-7367004-2-6

Published by FDI Publishing LLC. All rights reserved. Except for the purposes of fair reviewing, no part of this publication may be reproduced, distributed or transmitted in any form or by any means, or stored in a database or retrieval system, including by any means via the internet, without the prior written permission of the publisher. Infringers of copyright render themselves liable to prosecution.

———————

A division of FDI publishing LLC

geckos don't blink!

Other lizards blink.

Cats blink to say "I love you."

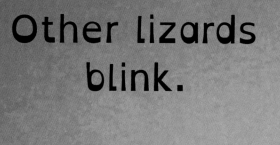

Ostriches blink every time they turn their head.

Can a gecko close their eyes to sleep?

No!
They hide their heads to sleep.

Can a gecko close their eyes to
sneeze?

No!
But their sneezes are adorable.

Can a gecko wink when they tell a joke?

Tee-hee, geckos don't tell jokes!

Why don't geckos blink?

They have no **eyelids!**

Eyelids are the skin that opens and closes over eyes.

Figure 1. Figure 2. Figure 3.
Open   Closed   Repeat

Eyelids can move fast, like blinking.

They can move one at a time, like winking.

Or they can stay closed, like when we sleep.

Blinking our eyelids keeps our eyes sparkling clean and moist.

If geckos don't blink, how do they keep their eyes clean and moist?

They lick them!

Geckos have really powerful eyes. They can see colors in the dark.

Color is important to geckos. Some geckos even have colorful eyes to help them blend in.

And that's the groovy thing about geckos.

Well, actually...

did you know there are over 1,500 types of geckos? And a few, like the leopard gecko, actually DO blink.

Whoa! That's crazy.

Get More *Awesome Animals* Books

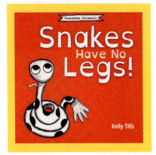  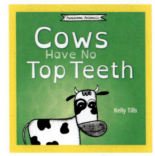 

About the Author

Kelly Tills writes silly books for kids and believes even the smallest hat-tip, in the simplest books, can teach our kids how to approach the world. Kelly's children's stories are perfect to read aloud to young children, or to let older kids read themselves (hey, let them flex those new reading skills!). Proud member of the *International Dyslexia Association*.

I hope this book brought you and your tiny human some fun time together. Help others find this book, and experience that same joy by **leaving a review!**

Point your phone's camera here.
It'll take you straight to the review page. Magic!

Made in United States
Orlando, FL
09 July 2023